I0443728

This book belongs to:

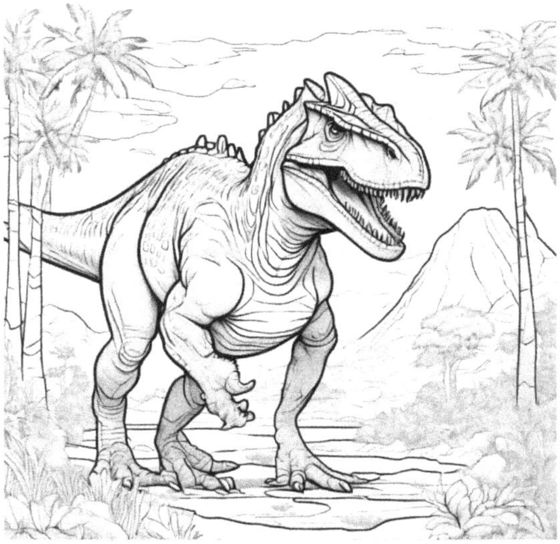

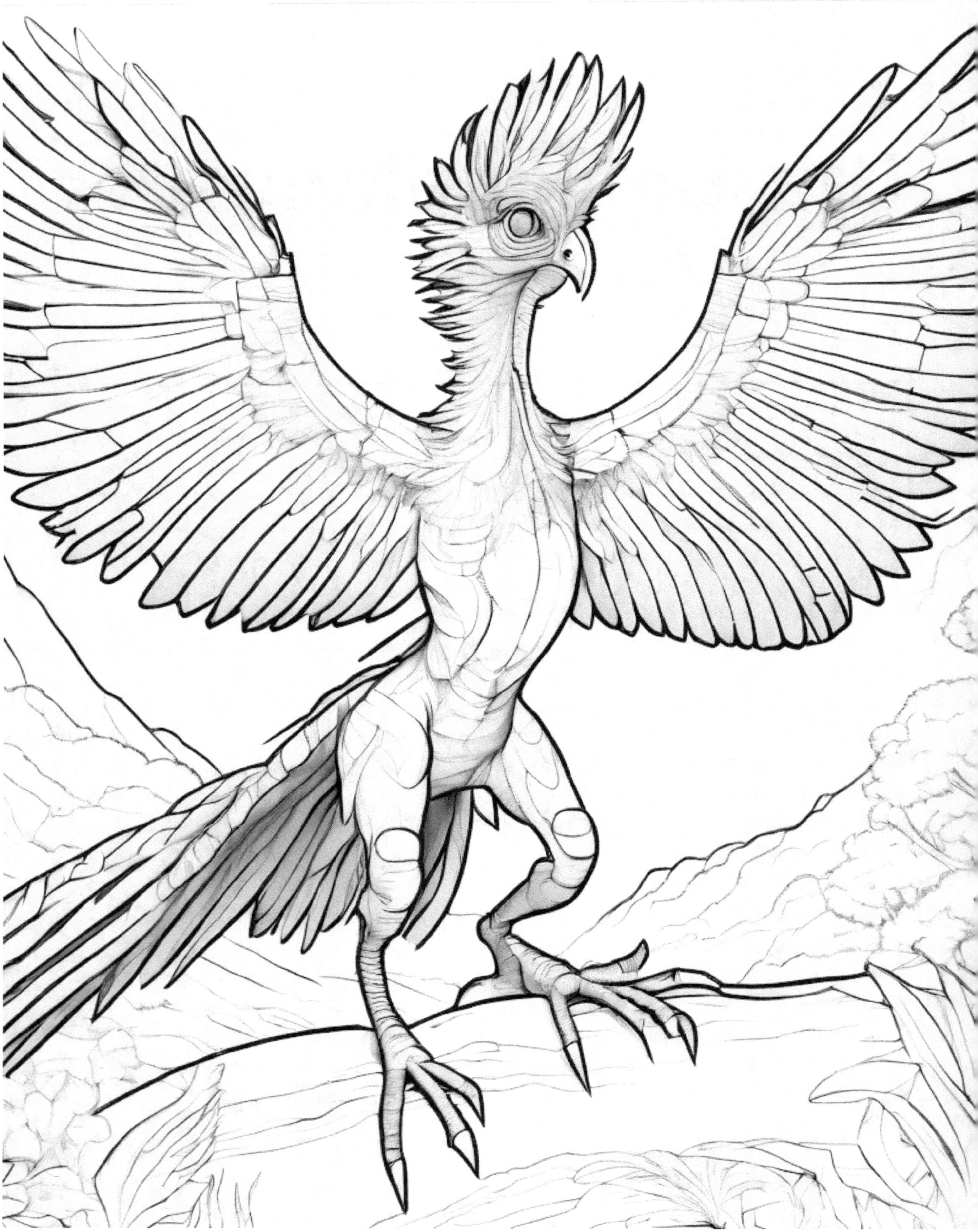

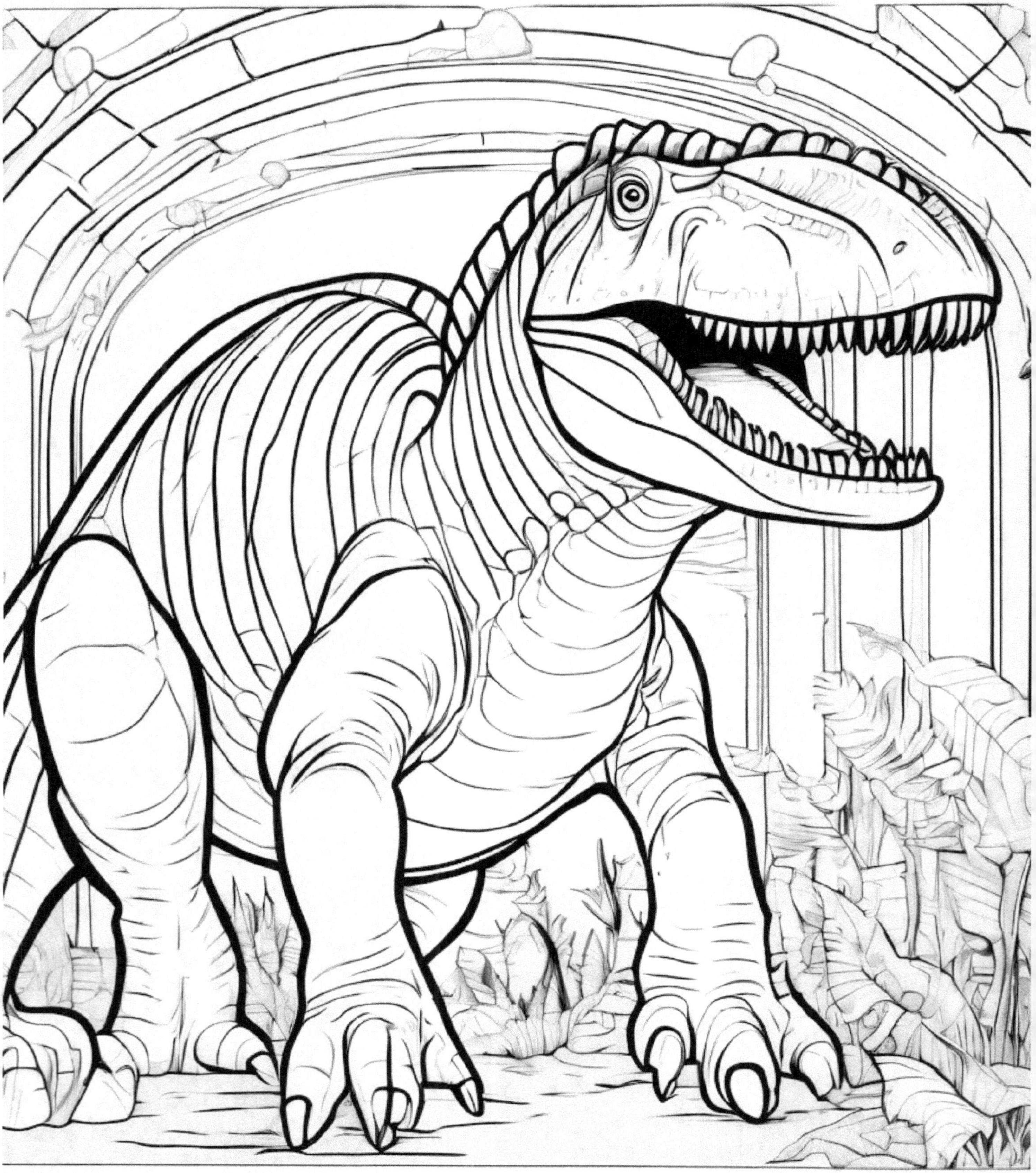

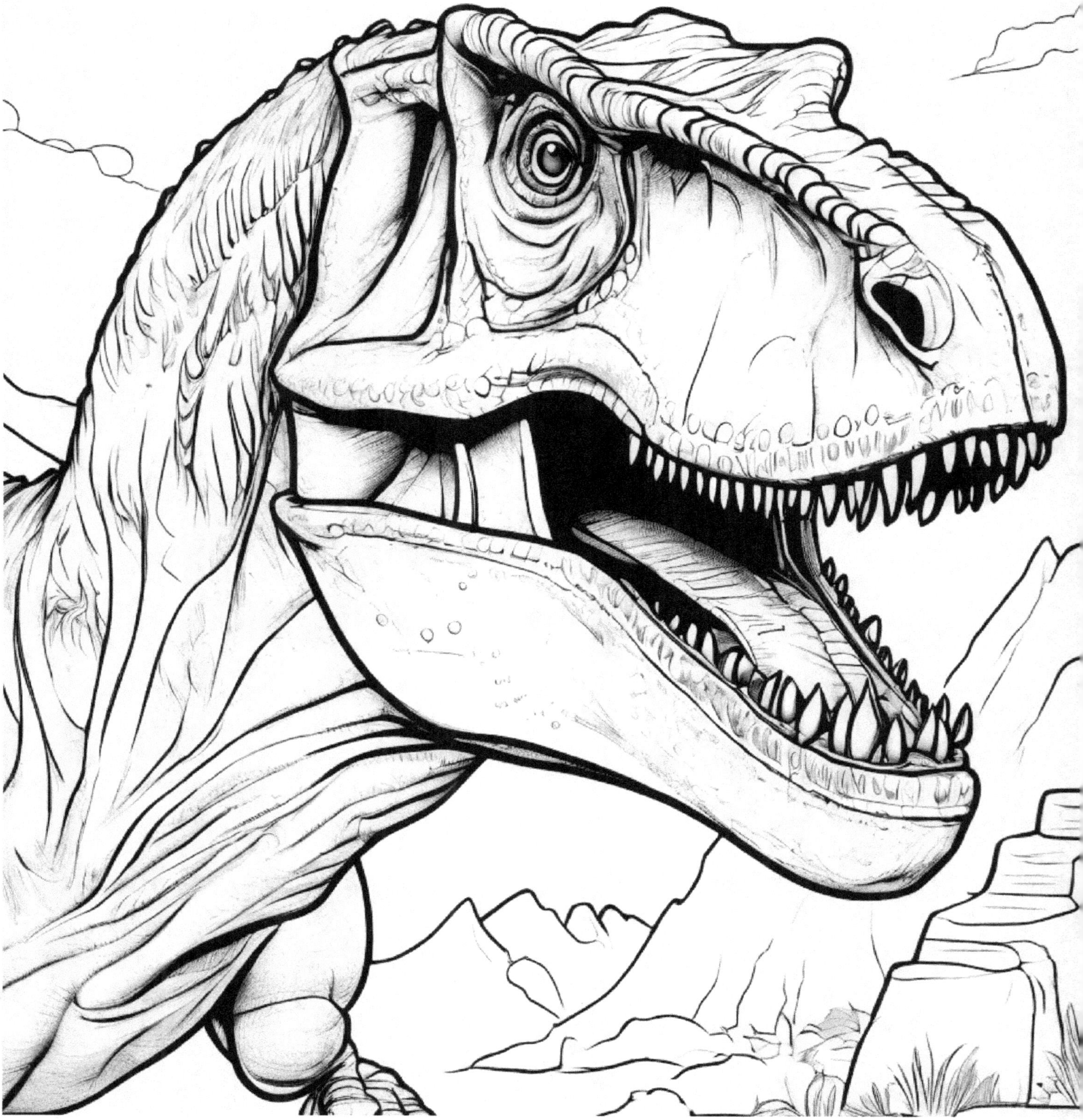

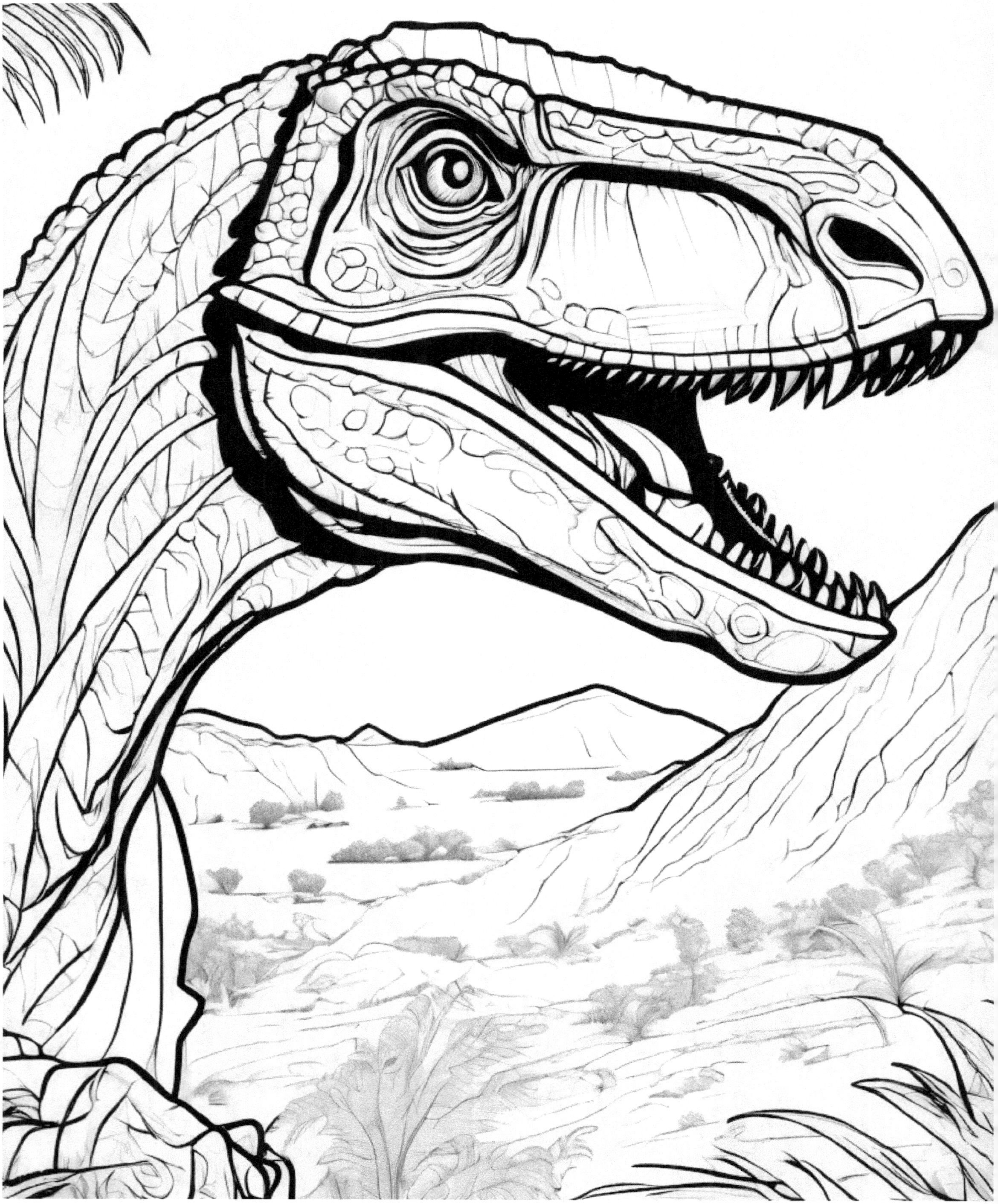

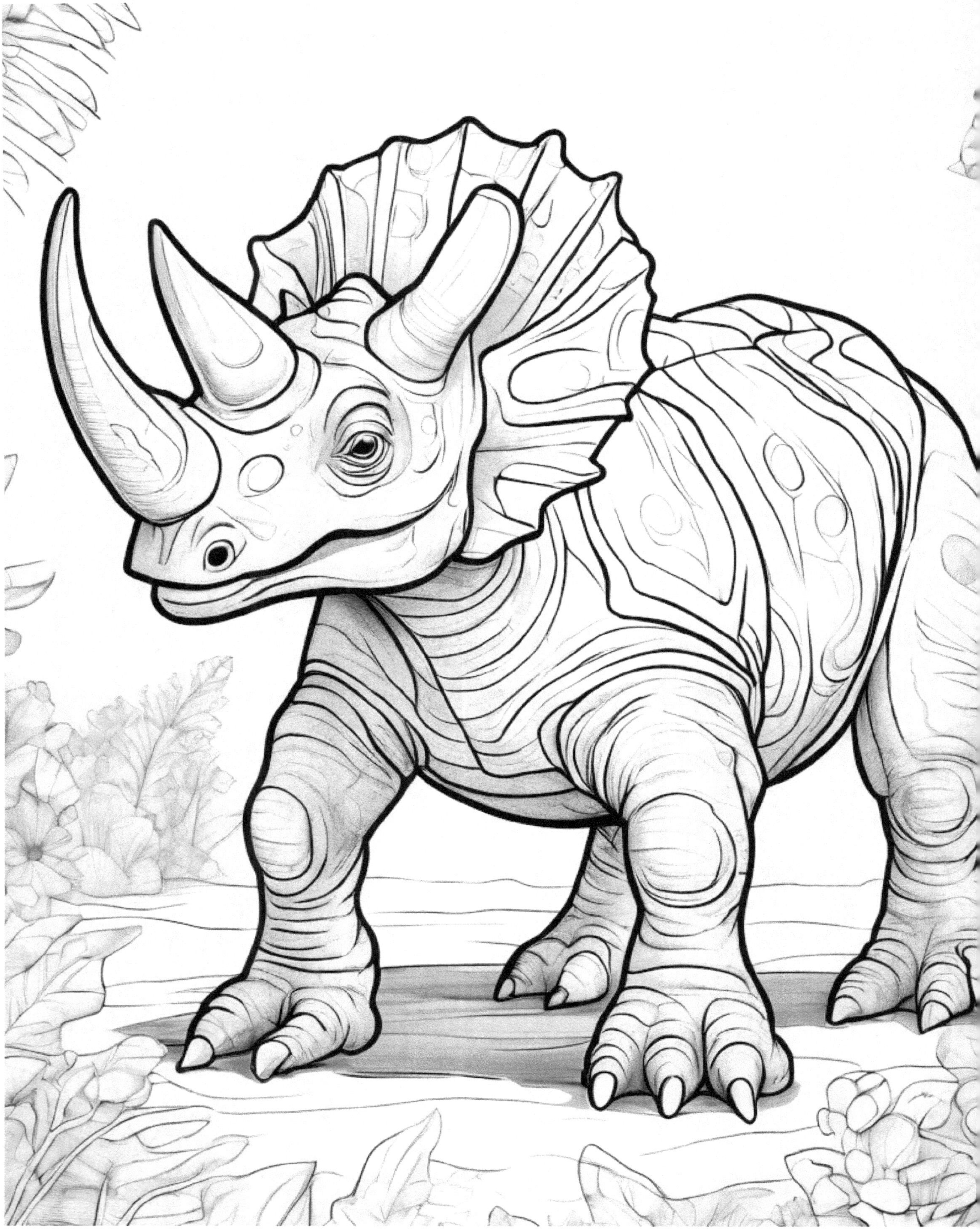

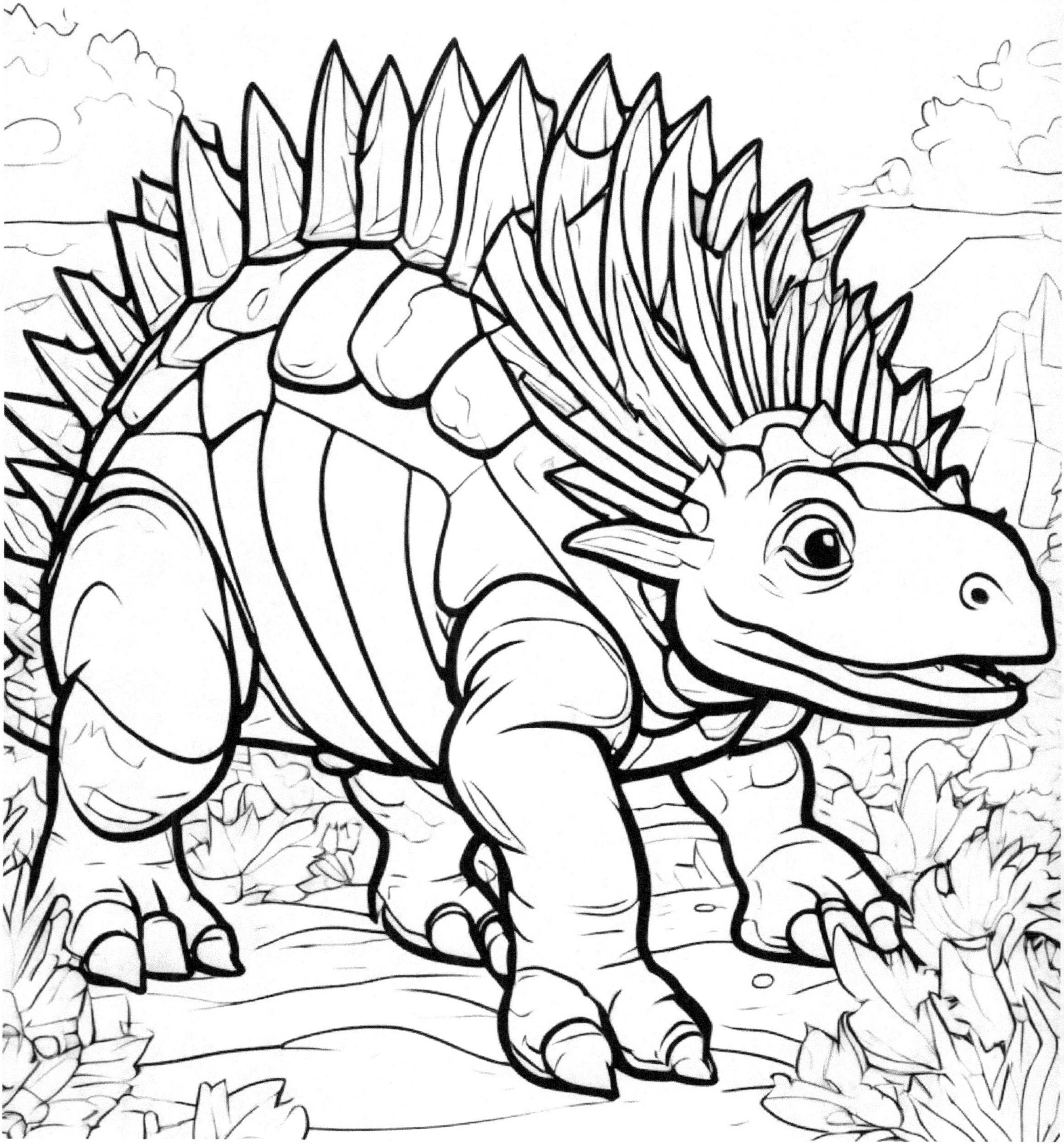

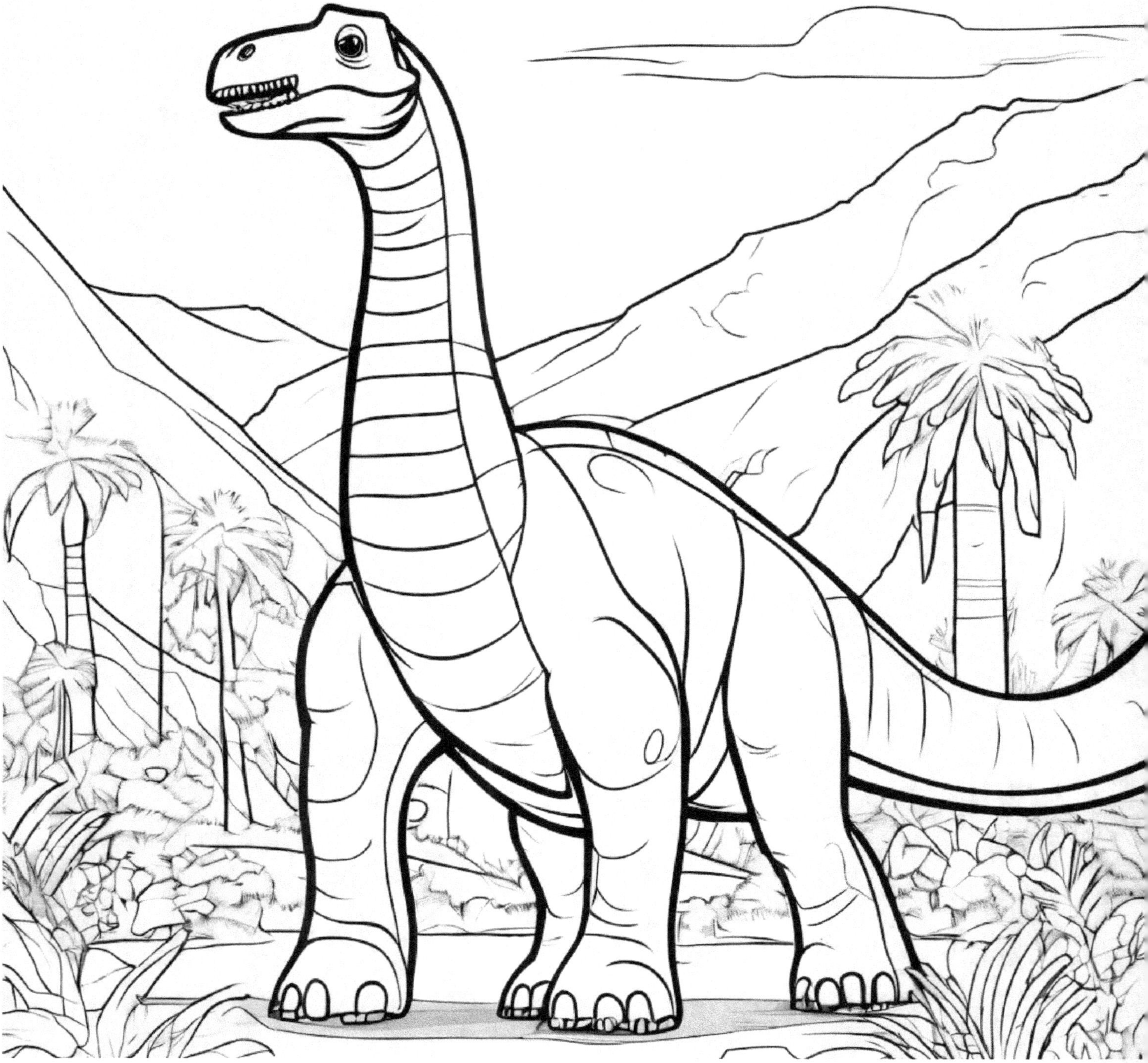

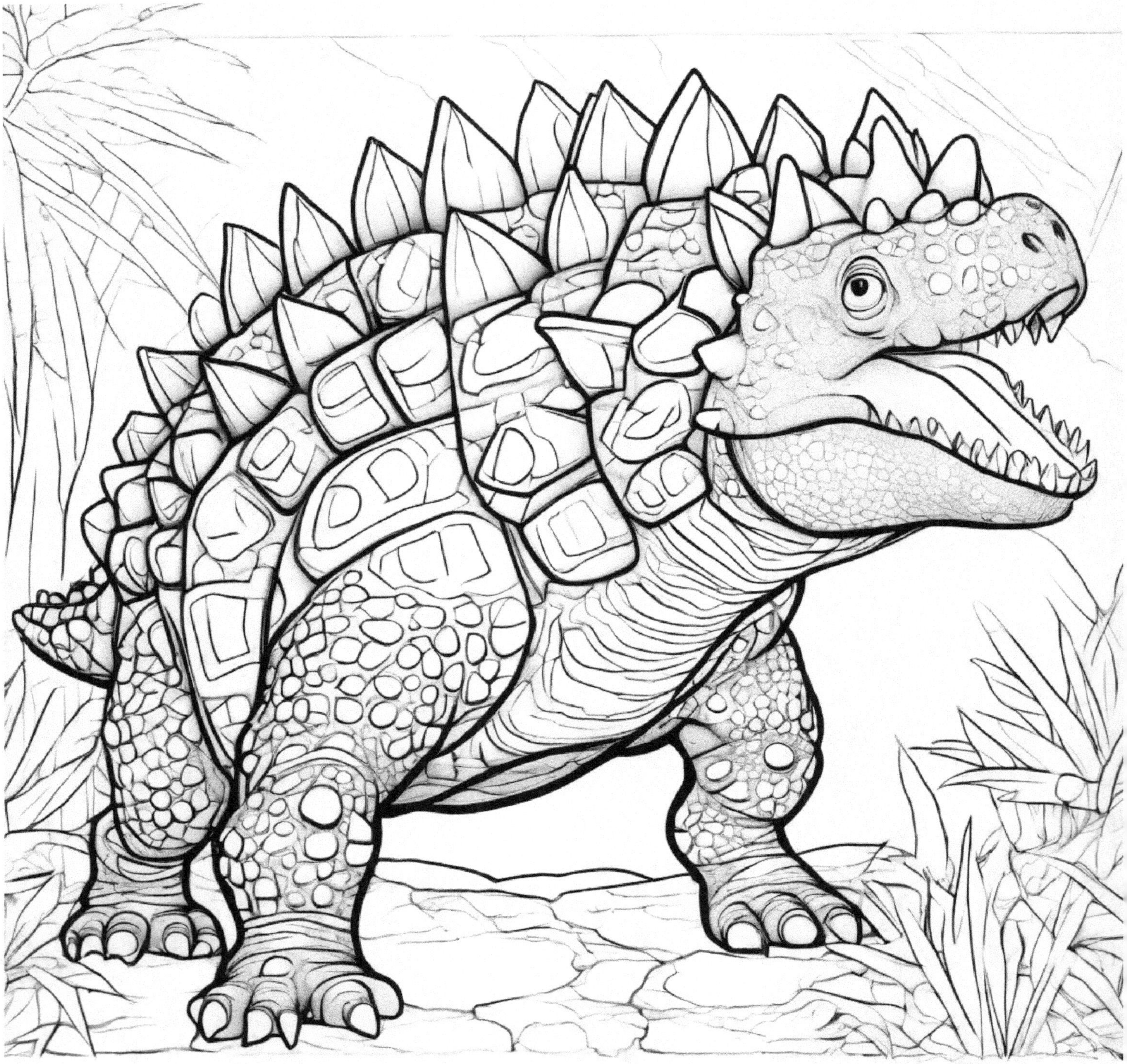

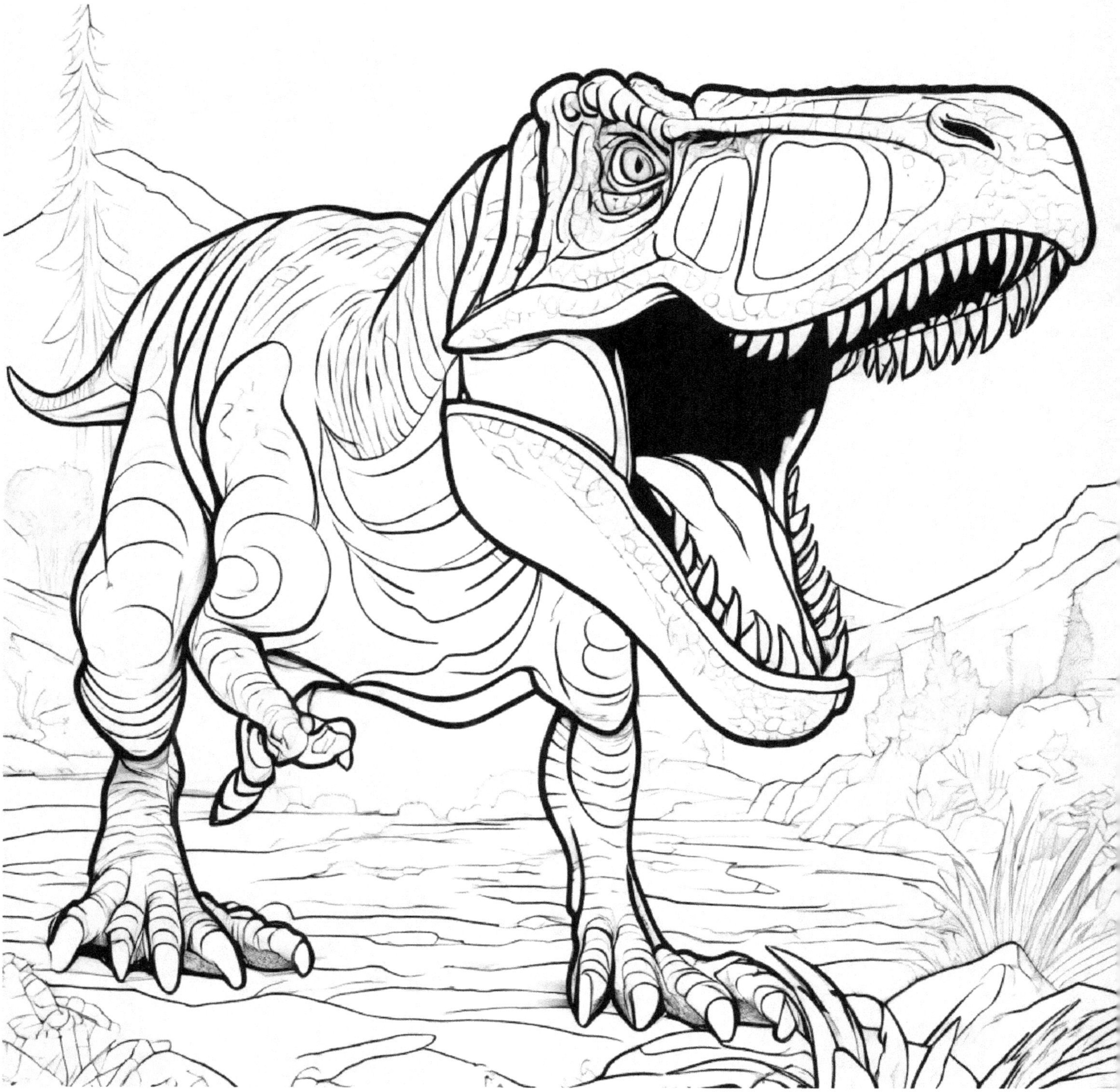

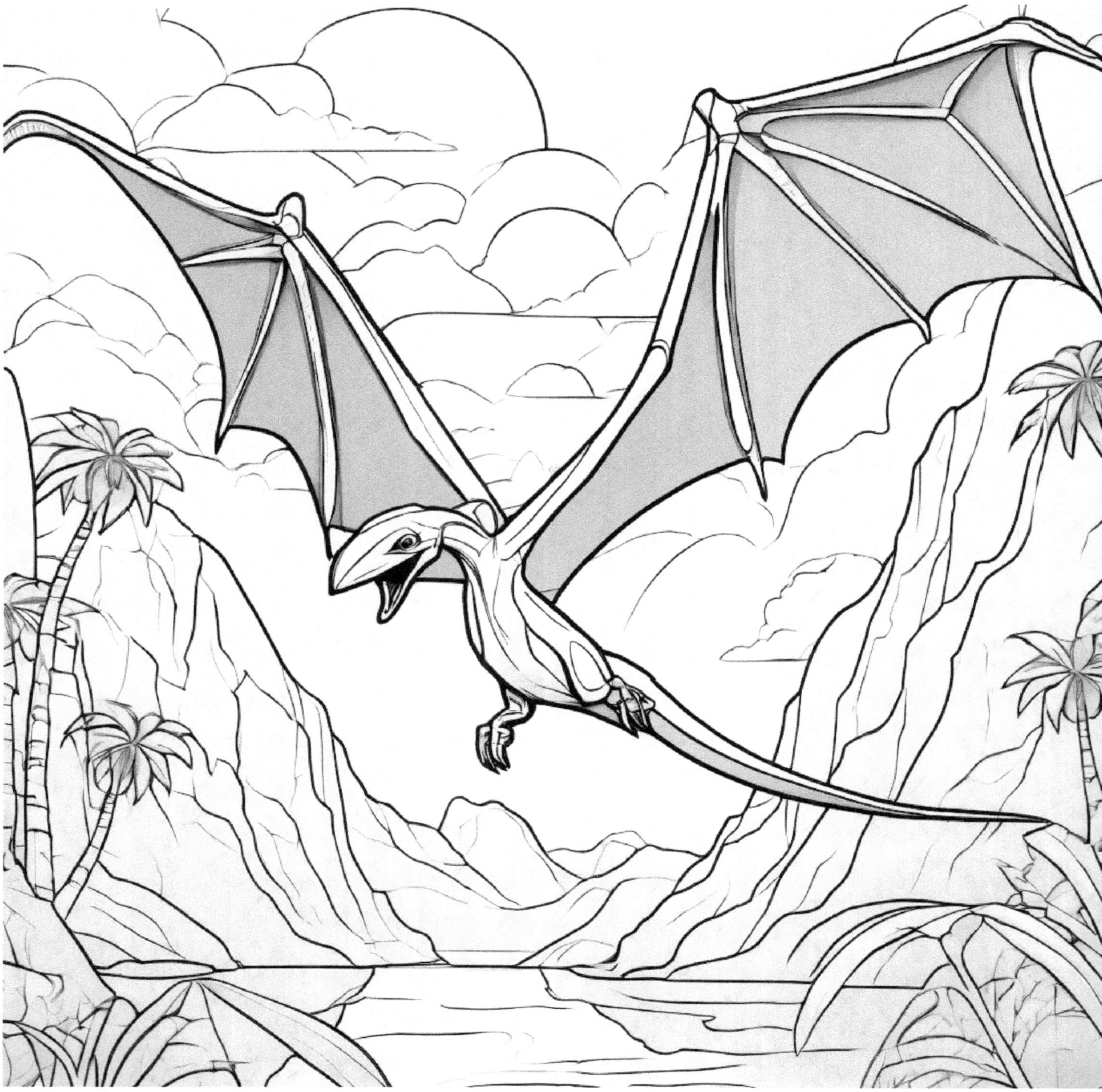

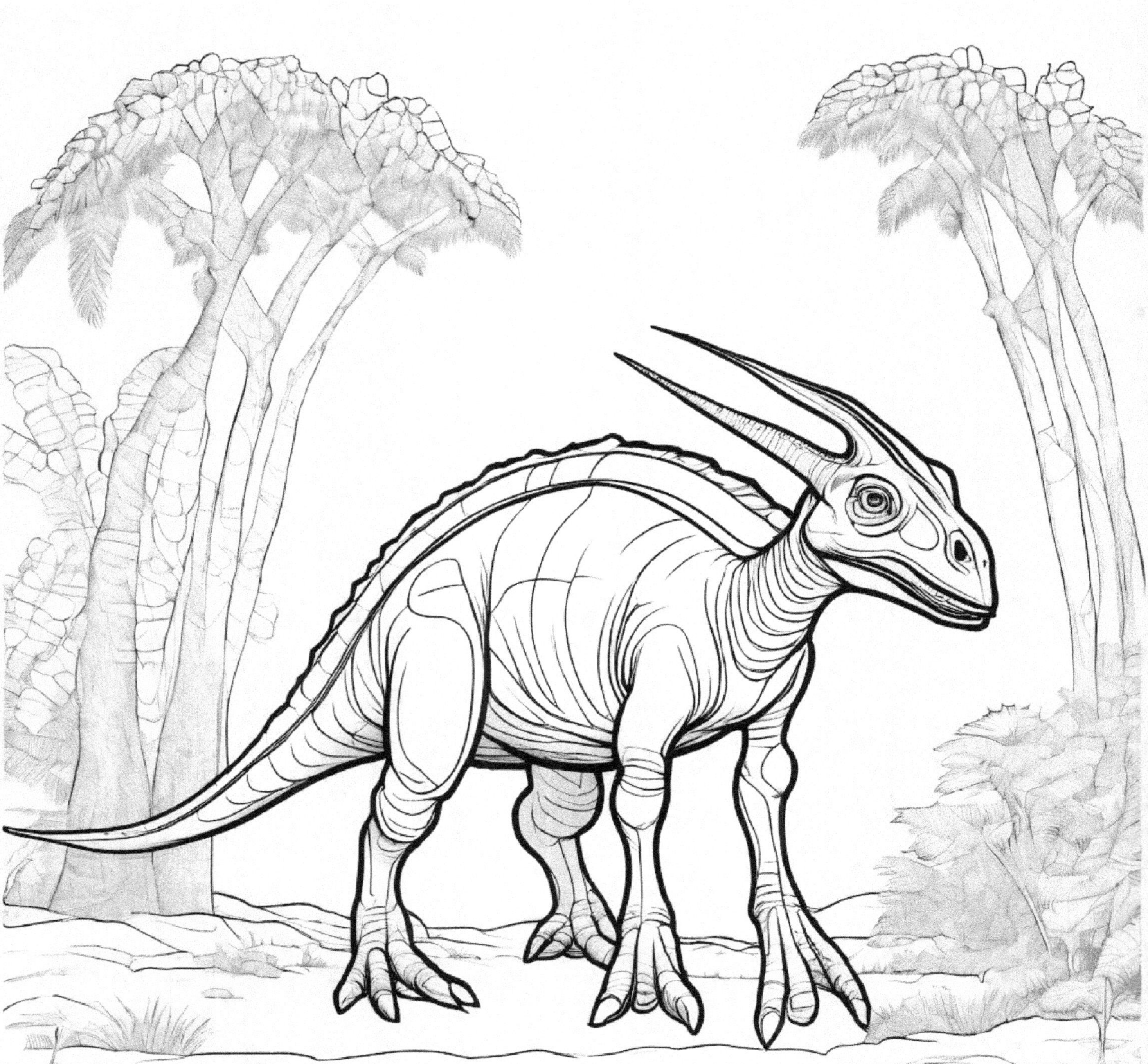

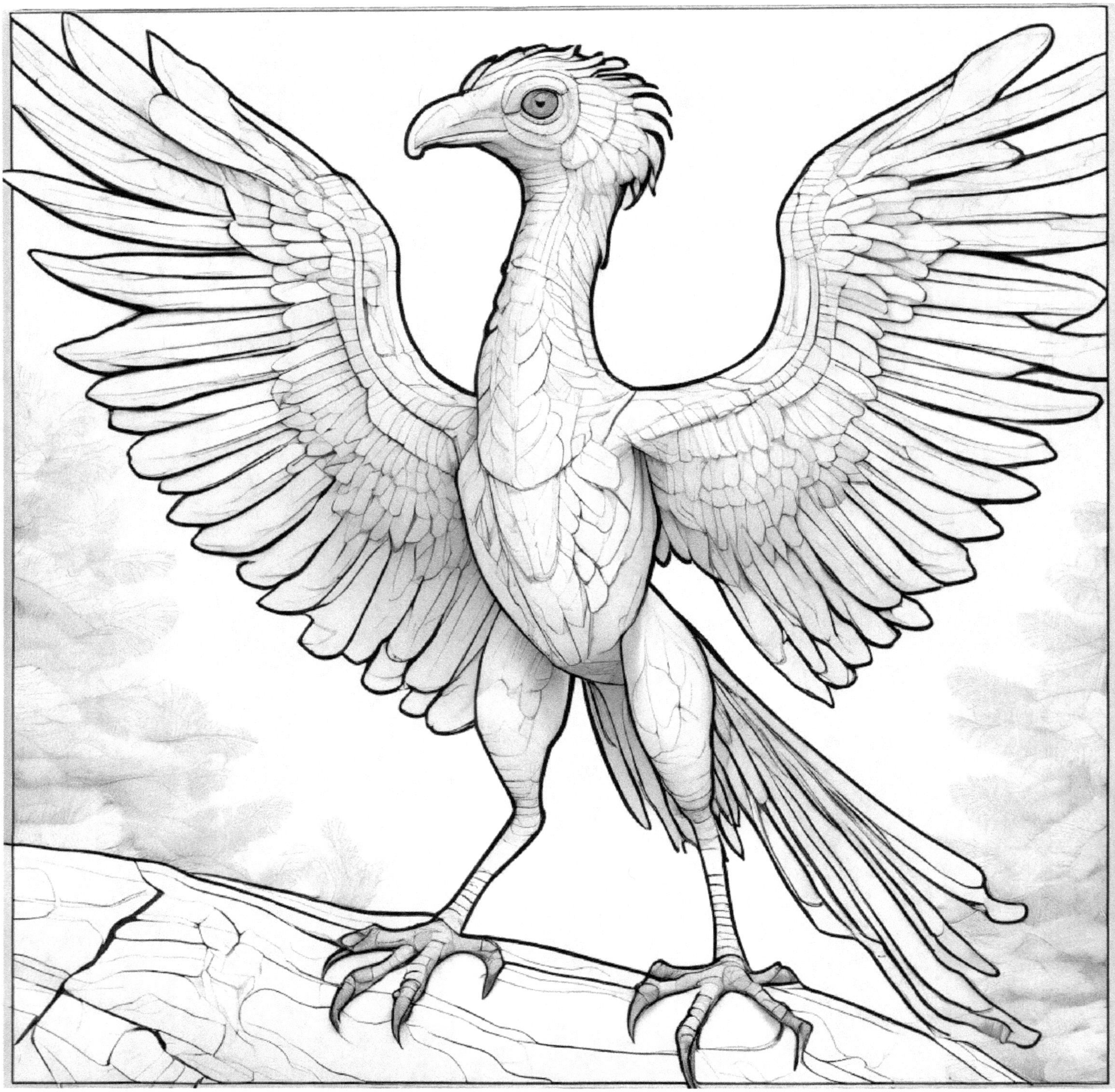

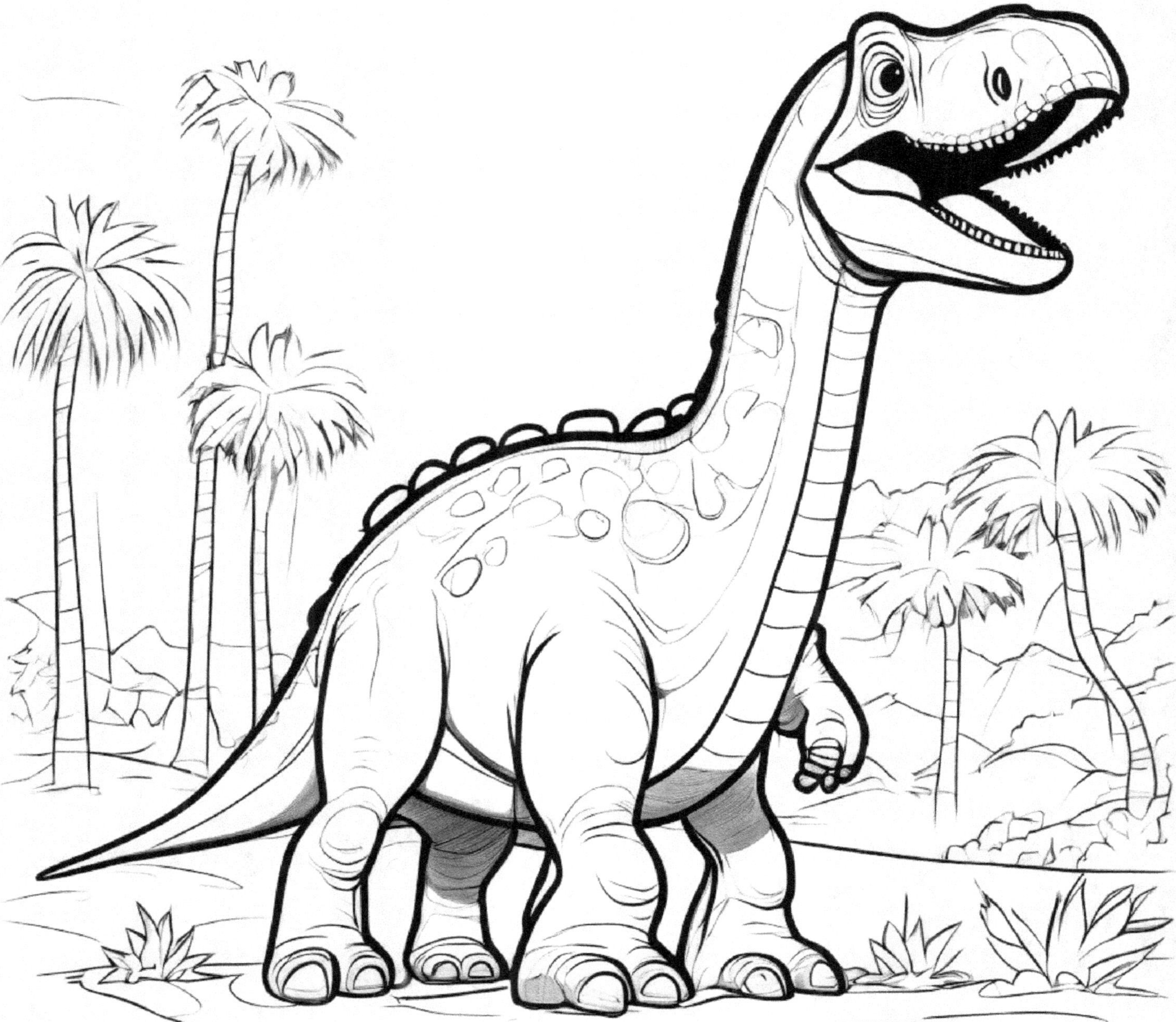

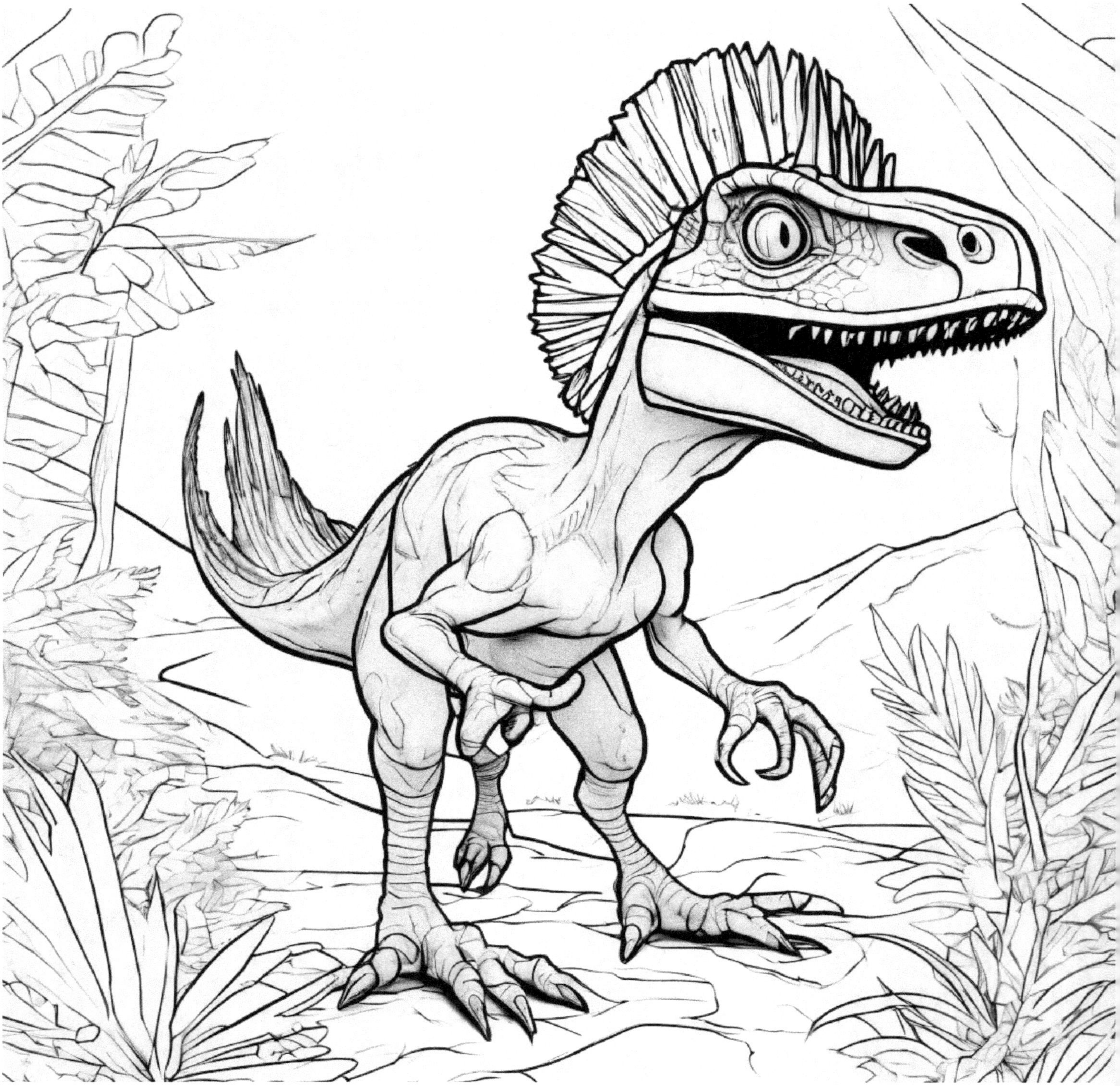

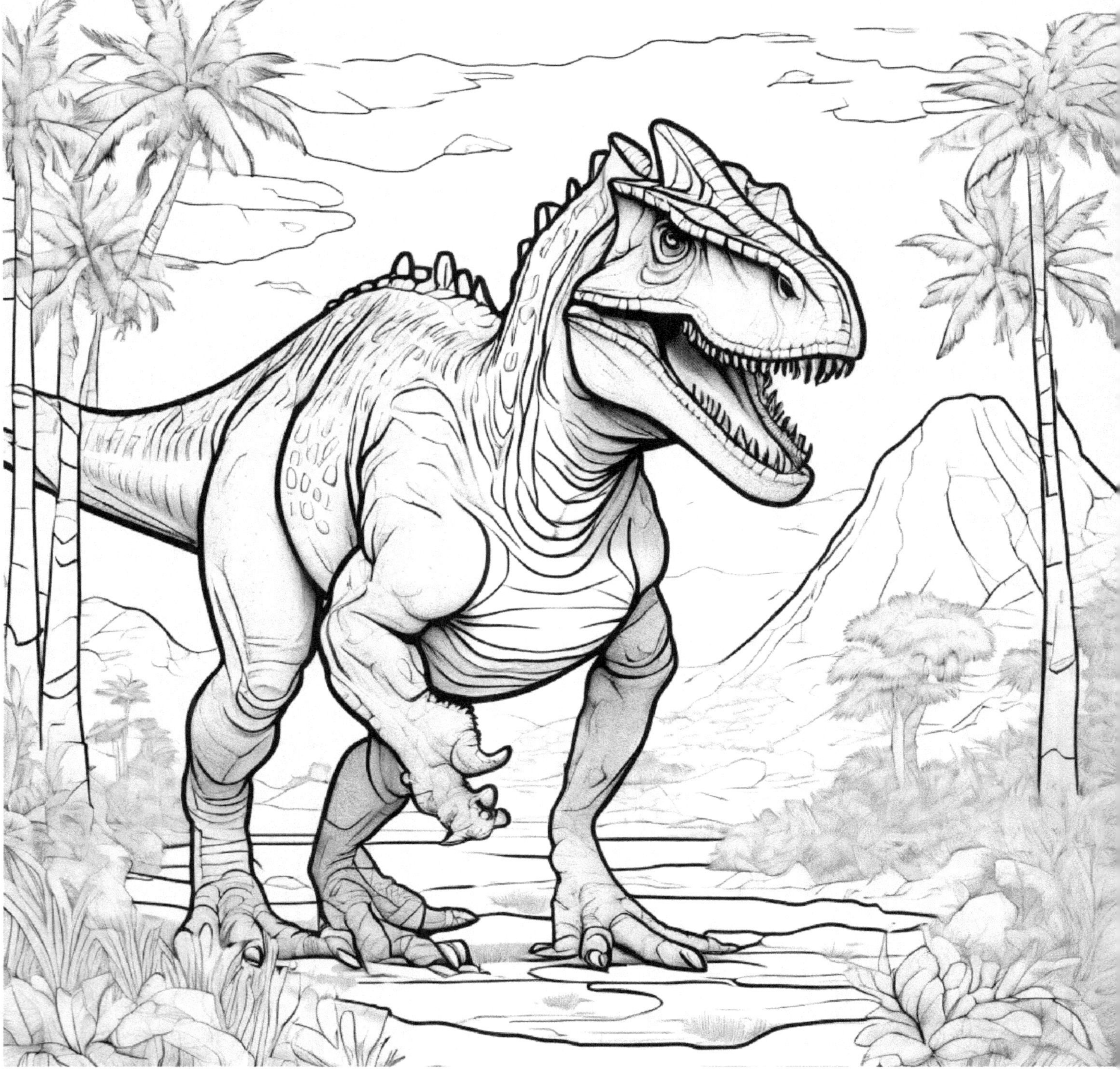

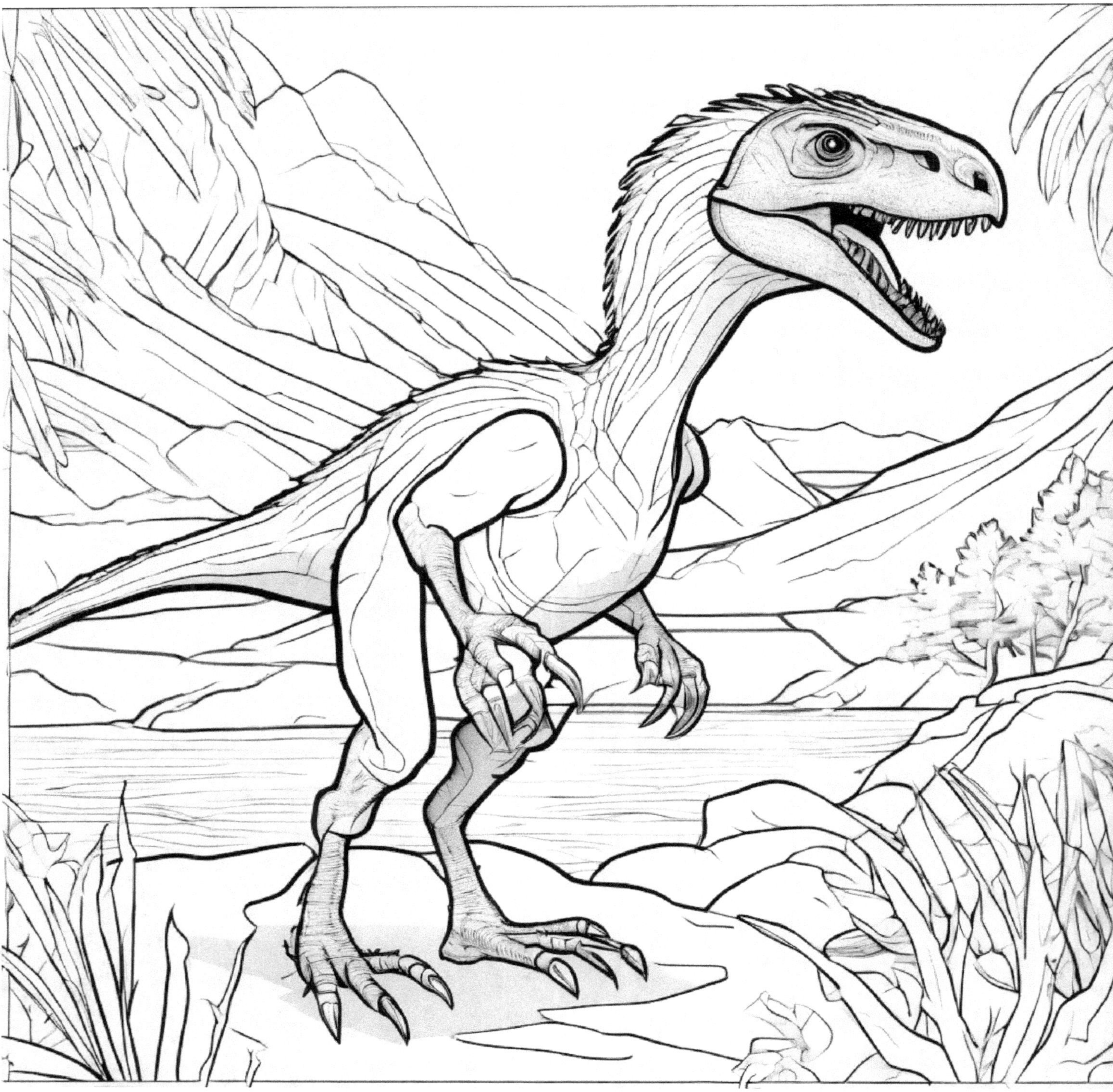

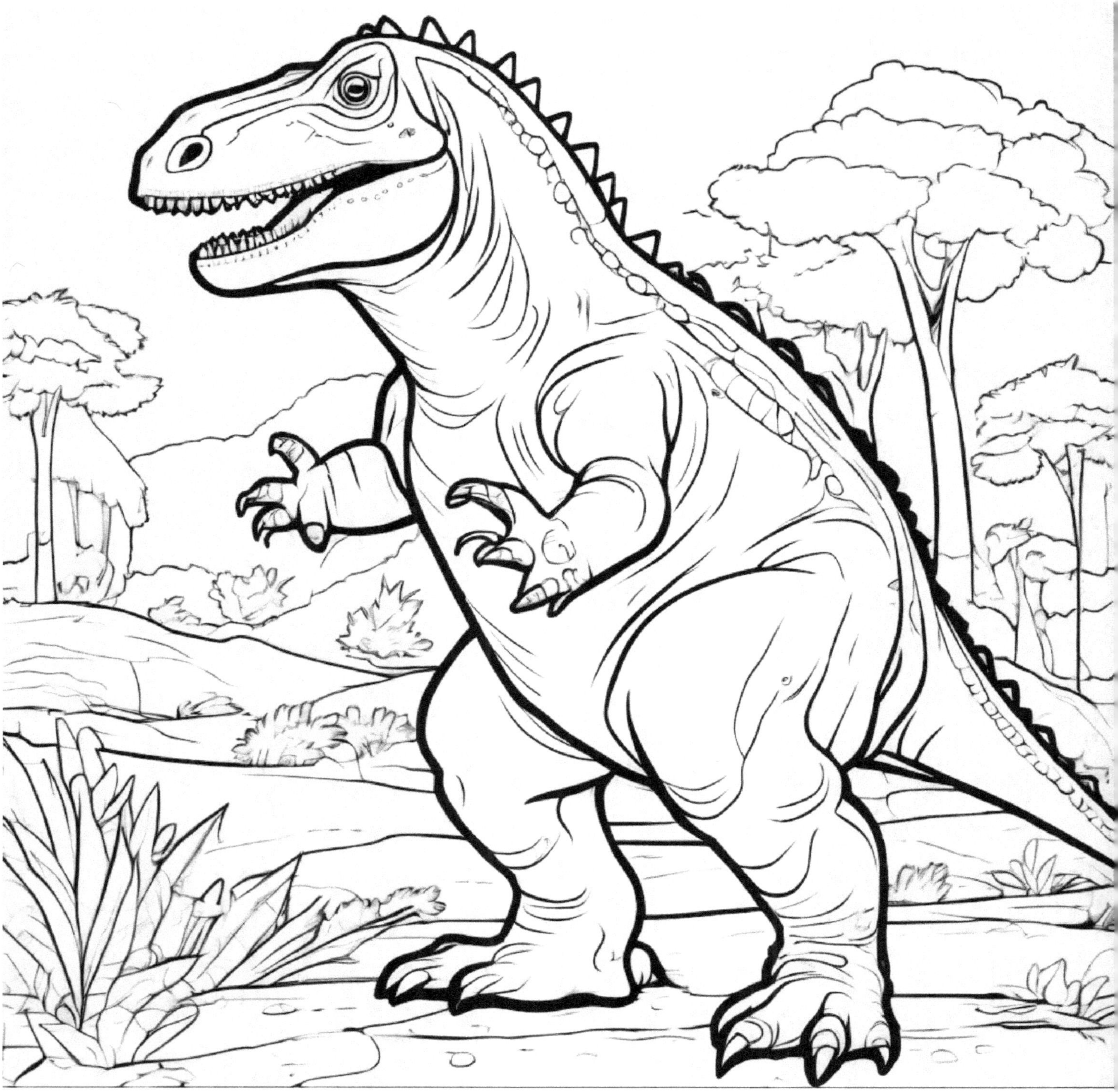

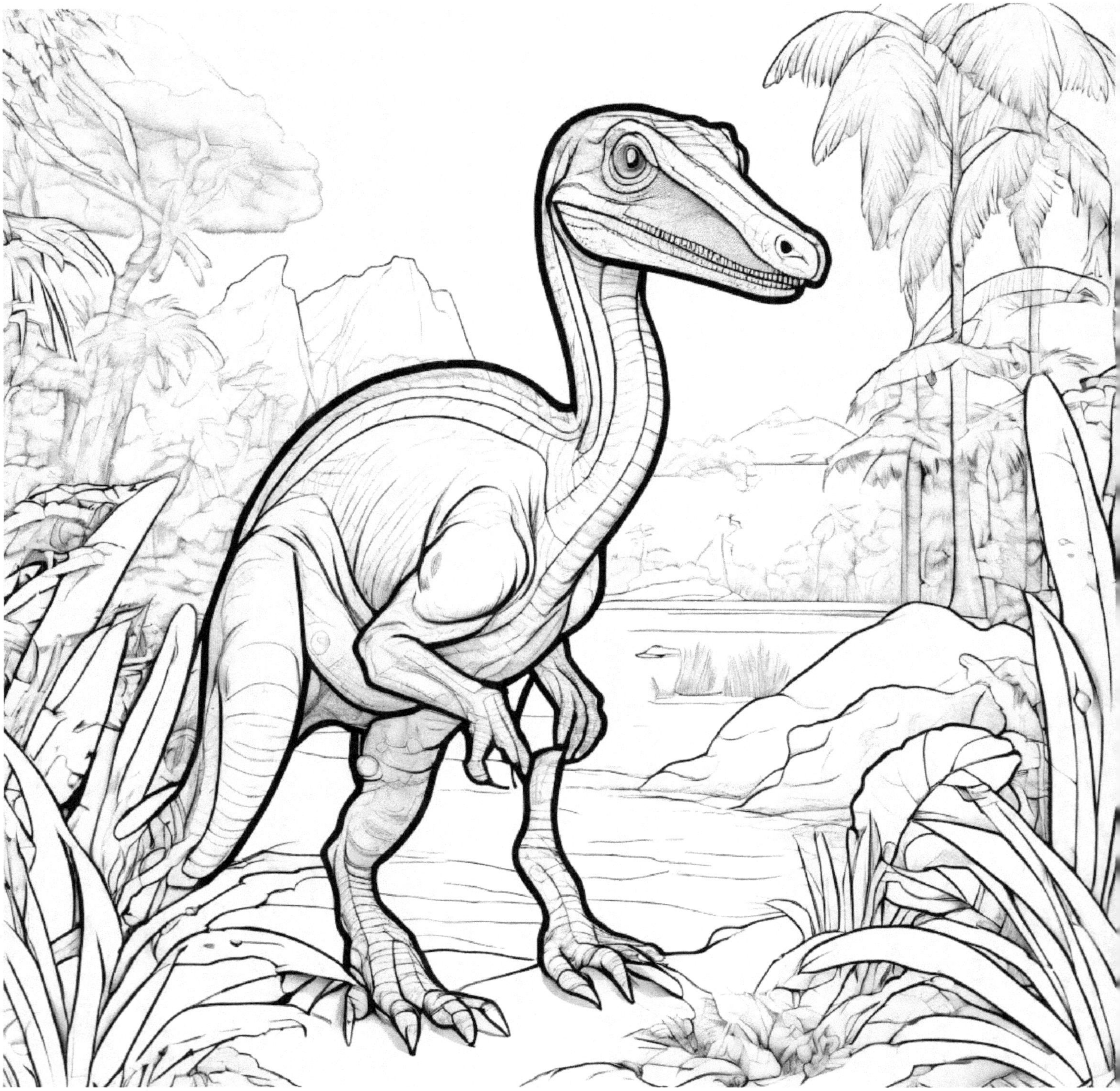

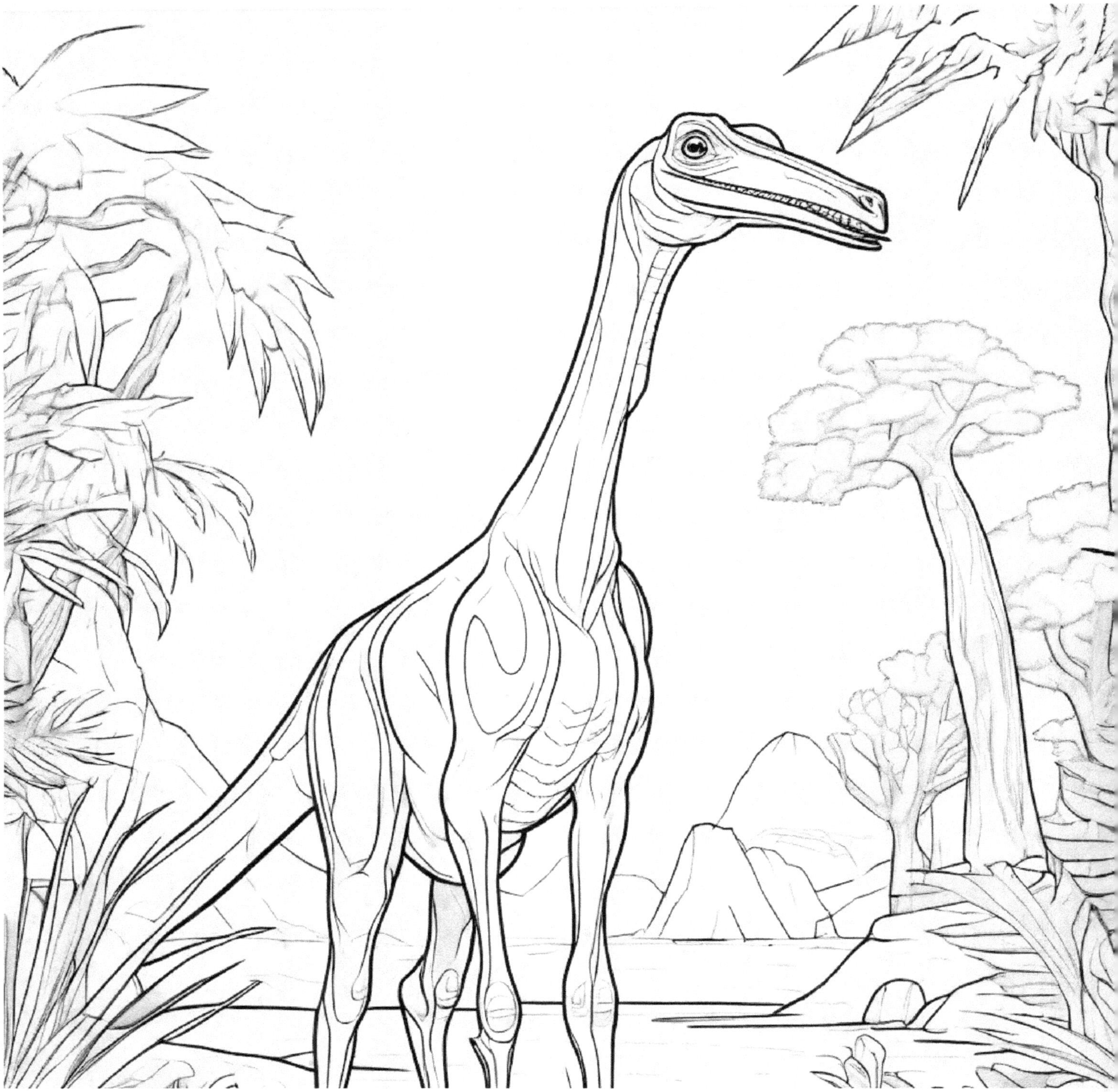

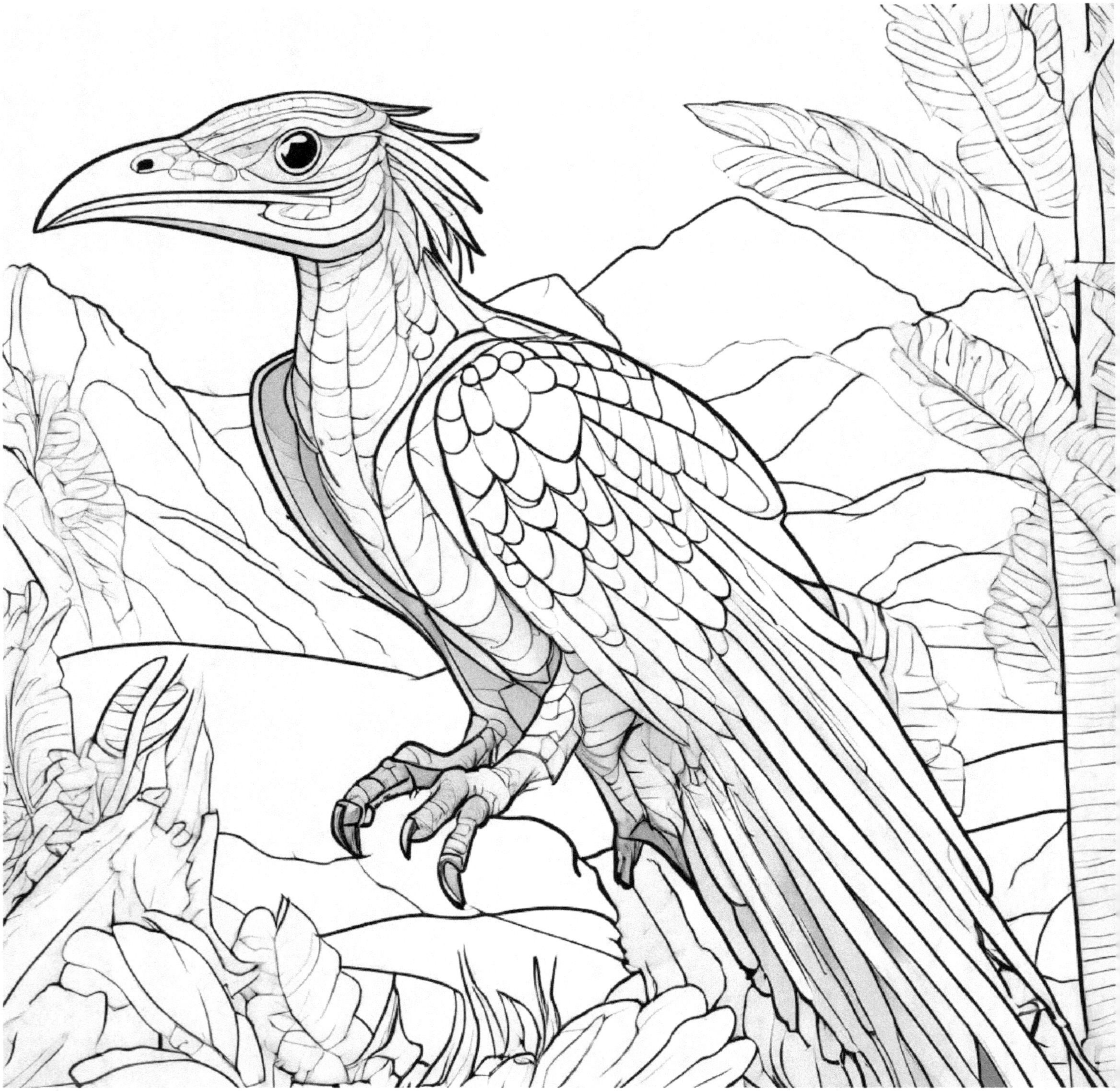

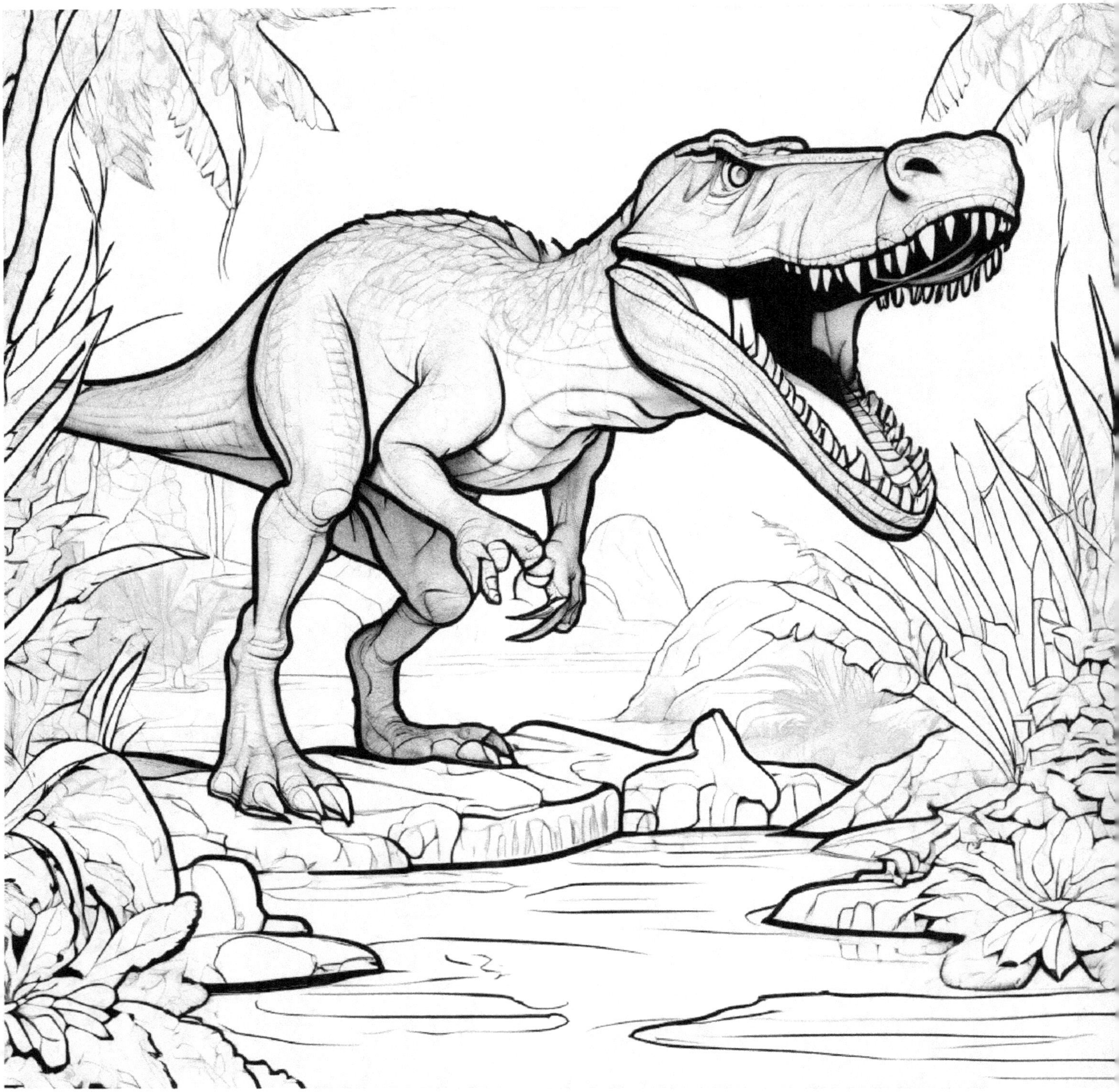

www.ingramcontent.com/pod-product-compliance
Lightning Source LLC
Chambersburg PA
CBHW082222220526
45470CB00010B/3276
9798324769468